LET'S ROCK

CRYSTALS

RICHARD AND LOUISE SPILSBURY

Chicago, Illinois

www.heinemannraintree.com
Visit our website to find out more information about Heinemann-Raintree books.

To order:
☎ Phone 888-454-2279
💻 Visit www.heinemannraintree.com to browse our catalog and order online.

Edited by Louise Galpine and Diyan Leake
Designed by Victoria Allen
Illustrated by Geoff Ward and KJA Artists
Picture research by Hannah Taylor
Originated by Capstone Global Library Ltd
Printed and bound in China by CTPS

14 13 12 11
10 9 8 7 6 5 4 3 2 1

Library of Congress Cataloging-in-Publication Data
Spilsbury, Richard, 1963–
  Crystals / Richard and Louise Spilsbury.
    p. cm. — (Let's rock)
  Includes bibliographical references and index.
  ISBN 978-1-4329-4684-5 (hb)
  ISBN 978-1-4329-4692-0 (pb)
  1. Crystals—Juvenile literature. 2. Crystallography—Juvenile literature. I. Spilsbury, Louise. II. Title.
  QD906.3.S65 2011
  549'.18—dc22   2010022241

Acknowledgments
The author and publisher are grateful to the following for permission to reproduce copyright material: Alamy Images pp. **16** (© PjrStudio), **18** (© imagebroker), **24** (© imagebroker); © Capstone Publishers pp. **28** (Karon Dubke), **29** (Karon Dubke); Corbis pp. **8** (Tony Waltham/Robert Harding World Imagery), **22** (dpa/Jens Wolf); FLPA p. **6** (Albert Lleal/Minden Pictures); Getty Images pp. **5** (Carsten Peter/Speleoresearch & Films/National Geographic), **15** (Per-Anders Pettersson), **23** (Imagemore Co., Ltd), **25** (Photo by Prudence Cuming Associates Ltd/DACS 2010), **26** (AFP/Matt Brown); istockphoto p. **13** (© KingWu); Photolibrary pp. **4** (A. & F. Michler), **11** (Gerhard Gscheidle), **12** (Imagebroker RF/Christian Handl), **14** (Alvaro Leiva), **17** (Thierry Bouzac), **20** (CuboImages/Alfio Giannotti), **27** (Peter Arnold Images/William Campbell).

Cover photograph of the Cave of Crystals (Cueva de los Cristales) in Naica Mine, Chihuahua, Mexico, reproduced with permission of Science Photo Library (MSF/Javier Trueba).

We would like to thank Dr. Stuart Robinson for his invaluable help in the preparation of this book.

Every effort has been made to contact copyright holders of any material reproduced in this book. Any omissions will be rectified in subsequent printings if notice is given to the publisher.

Disclaimer
All the Internet addresses (URLs) given in this book were valid at the time of going to press. However, due to the dynamic nature of the Internet, some addresses may have changed, or sites may have changed or ceased to exist since publication. While the author and publisher regret any inconvenience this may cause readers, no responsibility for any such changes can be accepted by either the author or the publisher.

CONTENTS

Rock roles

Find out about the work involved in the study of rocks.

Science tip

Check out our smart tips to learn more about rocks.

Number crunching

Discover the amazing numbers in the world of rocks.

Biography

Read about people who have made important discoveries in the study of rocks.

Some words are printed in bold, **like this**. You can find out what they mean by looking in the glossary on page 30.

WHAT ARE CRYSTALS?

Crystals are solid structures that have definite shapes with sharp, clear edges and corners. Salt, snowflakes, and rubies are types of crystal. The commonest crystals of all are those making up the rocks of our planet.

INSIDE ROCKS

Crystals are **minerals** that have had the chance and space to grow into a particular shape. Minerals are natural substances that formed inside or at the surface of Earth. If minerals form in spaces where there is not a lot of room, they may not have a crystal shape.

Science tip

Use a magnifying glass or microscope to look at grains of sugar and salt. See how light shines off their flat surfaces. Compare the shapes.

Snowflakes are ice crystals that form when droplets of water in clouds freeze.

CRYSTAL VARIETY

Some crystals are tiny, such as those inside granite rock. Other crystals are as long as a bus! Some crystals are common. **Quartz** crystals make up most of the sand on beaches and deserts around the world. Other crystals, such as sapphires, are rare. Diamonds are tough crystals that can be used to cut through metal. Other crystals, such as salt, **dissolve** in water or melt when heated.

In this book we will follow the story of crystals. We will discover how they form, what kinds there are, how we use them, and more . . .

The mineral **gypsum** is used to make plaster for walls. In 2000 miners discovered an underground cave full of enormous gypsum crystals. Some are more than 10 meters (32 feet) long and half a million years old.

HOW DO CRYSTALS FORM?

Most **minerals crystallize** (form crystals) from chemicals that are **dissolved** in liquid or present in hot, melted rock from inside Earth. But how?

CRYSTALS GROW

Crystals are packed with repeated rows of **atoms** or **molecules** (groups of atoms). Atoms are the tiny building blocks of everything on Earth. The atoms or molecules in a crystal pack together in a particular way, because each takes up a certain amount of space. Think of how eggs stack together in egg cartons. **Crystallization** starts with a tiny mineral crystal called the **seed crystal**. Then, more atoms or molecules of the same mineral attach, or link, to the outside of the seed, much like the way a magnet attracts pieces of metal.

These beautiful emeralds contain molecules made up of beryl, aluminum, silicon, and oxygen atoms.

LINKED TOGETHER

The strength of the links formed during crystallization affects a crystal's **properties**. For example, diamond and **graphite** are two minerals that contain only carbon atoms. In diamonds, each carbon atom is strongly and closely linked to four others. In graphite, each carbon atom is linked to three others in a layer, and the layers are linked weakly together. Graphite is used in pencil lead because layers can easily rub off onto paper, leaving a mark.

We know how crystals can grow and how their structure inside differs. But where does crystallization actually happen?

Diamond is harder than graphite because the atoms in its crystal are linked together more strongly.

Rock roles

Crystallographers are scientists who study crystals. Doctors use **X-rays** to see inside bodies. Crystallographers use X-rays to figure out the arrangement of atoms and molecules inside crystals!

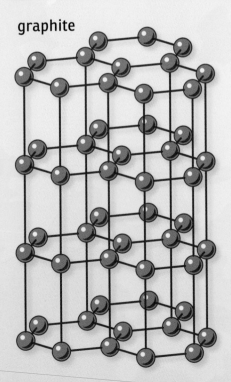

graphite

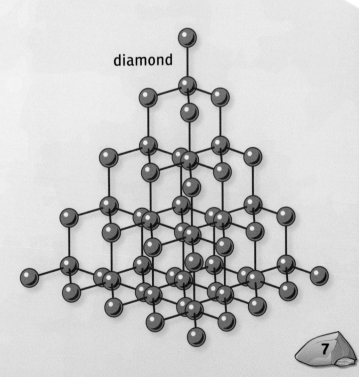

diamond

CRYSTALS FROM WATER

Have you ever seen white crystals around a dried-up rock pool? These crystallized from seawater. Seawater is a **solution**. It contains mostly salt and other minerals dissolved with water. Energy in heat and wind changes the solution. Liquid water in the solution changes into a gas called water vapor. This is called **evaporation**.

Evaporation leaves behind salt molecules that crystallize around salt seed crystals. Other minerals such as **gypsum** may also crystallize from other mineral-rich solutions at Earth's surface. However, many other crystals form underground.

Number crunching

If seawater 1 kilometer (3/5 mile) deep evaporated completely, it would leave a layer of salt crystals 15 meters (50 feet) deep!

In many places, such as Peru's Inca Salt Pans, people produce salt crystals for sale by putting seawater in shallow ponds to evaporate in the Sun's heat.

CAVE CRYSTALS

Some mineral solutions form when rainwater trickles underground from the surface. The water contains dissolved carbon dioxide from air. This makes the water **acidic**, so it can easily dissolve minerals from soft rocks, such as limestone. In some places, water has worn away so much limestone over long periods that underground caves have formed.

Water dripping through the roofs of caves contains the mineral **calcite** dissolved from the limestone rock. The calcite crystallizes when water evaporates from this solution. Sometimes crystals of calcite build up over time into amazing hanging structures called **stalactites**. The crystals may also grow into tall **stalagmites** where calcite solution splashes onto the floor of the cave.

Stalactites and stalagmites grow very slowly from minerals in dripping water. The fastest speed is around 3 mm ($^1/_{10}$ inch) a year.

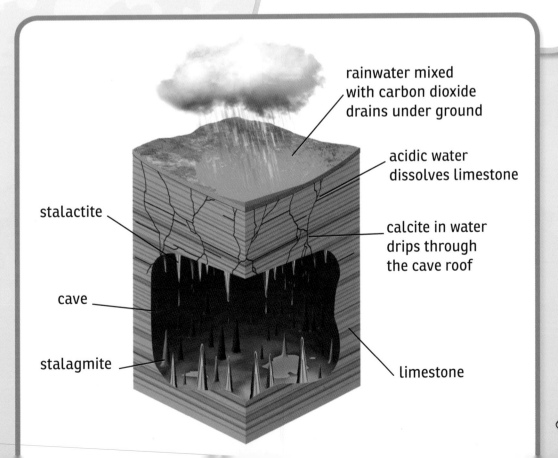

rainwater mixed with carbon dioxide drains under ground

acidic water dissolves limestone

calcite in water drips through the cave roof

stalactite

cave

stalagmite

limestone

CRYSTALS FROM HOT ROCKS

Many crystals grow when hot, liquid rock called **magma** finally cools. The hard, outer layer of surface rock on Earth is called the **crust**, and the thick layer of softer rock beneath is called the **mantle**. Magma mostly forms in the deepest parts of the mantle above the **core**, which is the (even hotter) center of Earth. Magma slowly moves around in the mantle all the time and sometimes comes up to the surface, where it cools.

Minerals can crystallize within the magma. They can also form solutions with underground water. The solutions seep into cracks in the magma, where they crystallize. This is why we sometimes find long **veins** of **quartz** crystal running through rocks.

The mantle, where many crystals form, is 2,900 km (1,800 miles) thick. The solid iron inner core of Earth crystallized from the iron-rich magma in the outer core.

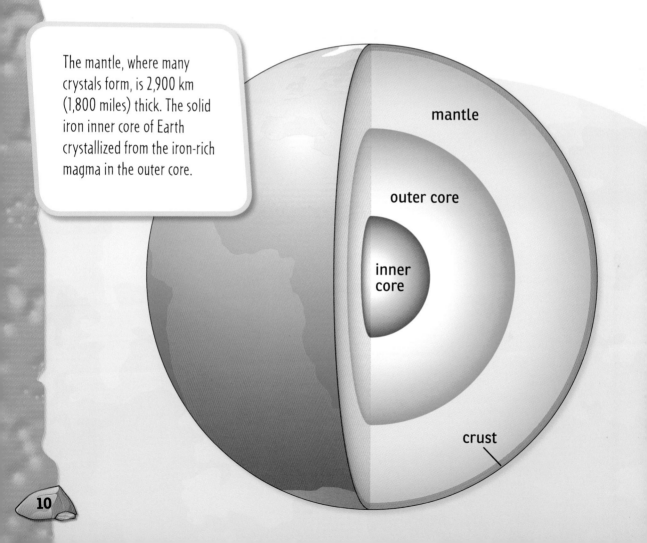

mantle

outer core

inner core

crust

DEEPEST CRYSTALS

Most diamond crystals worn as jewelry today first grew 150 kilometers (93 miles) underground, deep in the mantle. That is 16 times deeper than Mount Everest is high! The weight of thousands of tons of rock above creates high **pressure**. The pressure causes melted carbon in the magma to crystallize into tough diamonds. In lower-pressure conditions, the carbon would have formed graphite.

Rock roles

Some **geologists** develop special machines that can create high pressures and high temperatures just like in the mantle. They use them to study the conditions that can make crystals form or melt, and even to make diamonds.

Diamonds are found in Earth's crust because rising magma has carried them there from the mantle, where they formed.

WHERE DO WE FIND CRYSTALS?

Geologists use their knowledge about rocks and **crystallization** to help look for crystals. We find some crystals where they are exposed on Earth's surface, but most are hidden underground.

CRYSTAL LOCATIONS

Geologists look for crystals in certain types of rock or in particular places. For example, most diamonds are found in kimberlite rock, formed when deep **magma** rose to the surface and cooled. Some crystals are mostly found near **volcanoes**, where magma comes near or up to the surface through gaps in Earth's **crust**. For example, **sulfur** crystals grow where hot magma or volcanic gas rich in sulfur **minerals** cools down.

Sulfur crystals have a distinctive bright-yellow color and smell faintly of rotten eggs! People collect sulfur to make things such as rubber and matches.

The dramatic peaks in Guilin, China, were formed by weathering and erosion of minerals in limestone.

WORN AWAY

Most crystals are revealed when surface rock is broken up into **particles** (tiny pieces) by **weathering** or **erosion**. This happens over long periods of time and in different ways. It can happen when water freezes in cracks in rocks and forces them open. Crystals of harder minerals may be left behind when rock is carried away by wind or flowing water.

Rock roles

Sedimentologists study sedimentary rocks. They use clues in the particles to figure out the weathering and erosion history of Earth.

Weathering and erosion are part of the **rock cycle**, in which rocks continuously change from one type to another. Over millions of years, weathered particles of **mantle** form new rock called **sedimentary rock** in Earth's crust. In some places on Earth, this crust sinks into the mantle, where its minerals melt into magma.

SEPARATING CRYSTALS

People separate crystals from unwanted particles in different ways. One way is to spray water from high-**pressure** hoses at hard soil that might contain crystals. The force breaks up the soil and the particles mix with water, making thin mud. The mud is then filtered through a sieve to remove any crystals.

Science tip

Find a shallow stream with a gravel bottom. Check with an adult that it is safe to step into. Scoop up gravel using an old, flat frying pan and swirl it in a circle. You should find that gravel washes away, but heavier objects of the same size, such as crystals, remain in the pan.

In some places, people swirl gravel from river beds using pans or baskets to separate out crystals.

MINING CRYSTALS

Sometimes miners find solid **veins** of crystals sticking out of surface rocks. Miners in the past used hard deer antlers and axes to chip off crystals. They gradually dug underground using spades, following the vein. Today, miners use powerful digging machines and drills to dig underground in search of crystals. They create tunnels held open with strong metal supports so that they can continue mining deeper and deeper.

The rock that the miners dig out sometimes contains crystals hidden inside it. The miners crush the rock into sludge to get at the crystals. Diamond miners pour crushed kimberlite rock sludge down a slope covered in grease. Only the diamonds stick to the grease.

This enormous diamond mine in Botswana is the biggest in the world. Each one of the trucks in the picture can hold over 200 tons of rock that might contain diamonds!

MAKING CRYSTALS

Some scientists do not need to find or mine crystals, because they grow their own! Usually they grow crystals from strong mineral **solutions** inside heated machines. The conditions are controlled so that scientists can make sure the crystals grow big and have no cracks. For example, long crystals of **silicon** are grown so that they can be cut into thin slices and used in solar cells to make electricity from sunlight.

Rock roles

Some people make cheap, fake **gemstones** to sell. Geologists sometimes work for jewelers or law enforcement officers to spot fake crystals. They look for differences in **properties** between genuine and fake crystals. For example, **laser** light moves differently through a real diamond than a fake one.

Zirconia crystals are made in laboratory machines. They are far cheaper and sparkle even more than diamonds.

COLLECTING CRYSTALS

Would you like to collect your own crystals? Visit a local library or museum to find an area near you where it is safe to look for interesting crystals. Wear old clothes and gloves when you are collecting, to avoid getting dirty or being hurt by sharp rocks. You will often need to break rocks open to uncover crystals. Always wear goggles to stop rock chips or dust from getting in your eyes, and use a special rock hammer. The metal used for normal hammers can shatter against harder rocks.

Science tip

Beware of sulfur crystals! Breathing in fumes from these can damage your lungs. People who work in sulfur mines wear special masks to protect them from the fumes.

These people are mining sulfur from a volcano in Java, Indonesia.

WHAT TYPES OF CRYSTAL ARE THERE?

There are over 3,000 types of **mineral** on Earth. How can we tell their crystals apart?

SIZE AND SHAPE

Crystals come in different sizes and shapes, partly depending on the conditions where they grow. For example, the **gypsum** crystals on page 5 grew enormous because for centuries they were bathed in a strong gypsum **solution** and had space to grow. Elsewhere on Earth, gypsum crystals are smaller because growing conditions were different. The shapes also depend on the way different minerals **crystallize**. For example, hematite crystals often crystallize in shapes that look like bunches of grapes!

Geodes are spaces in rocks where crystals like this amethyst quartz grow inward from the edge.

REGULAR SHAPE

The arrangement of **atoms** inside crystals gives them a regular shape with flat sides, or faces, on the outside. The shapes are **symmetrical**. This means that the faces on one side are the same as those on the opposite side. **Geologists** use six general crystal shapes (see diagram) to identify crystals. For example, **quartz** grows into a six-sided column shape, but garnets form cubes.

Biography

Rene-Just Haüy (1743–1822) was a French priest and geologist. Around 1790 he accidentally dropped a **calcite** crystal, and it broke into small, regular pieces. Haüy studied the pieces and realized that crystal shapes depend on what they are made from. He wrote the first book about the shapes and **properties** of crystals in 1801.

The lines inside these crystal shapes show where they could be cut into equal halves. These are the lines of **symmetry**.

cubic	tetragonal	hexagonal	orthorhombic	monoclinic	triclinic
examples: halite, garnet, galena	examples: zircon, wulfenite, chalcopyrite	examples: quartz, calcite, beryl	examples: **sulfur**, olivine, barite	examples: mica, gypsum, azurite	examples: **feldspar**, rhodonite, kyanite

CRYSTAL COLORS

We can identify some crystals by their color. For example, lazurite is always blue. However, other crystals are found with different colors. Beryl crystals can be green, blue, yellow, pink, or clear, depending on what atoms were present when they formed. Alexandrite crystals are a different color in electric lamp light than they are in daylight.

Science tip

Look through a transparent crystal at a page in a book. How do the words look? Some crystals, such as peridot, make a double reflection of each word because they can bend light. It is a little like the way a straw looks bent in a glass of water. This is because light moves differently through water than it does through air.

Different crystals glow with different colors when we shine a special light called ultraviolet on them. This is another useful test for identifying crystals.

CLEAR DIFFERENCES

Different types of crystal may have the same color, while one type of crystal may come in different colors, so geologists use tests to tell them apart. For instance, they test a crystal's hardness by what can scratch it, using fingernails, different metals, or even other crystals. Diamond is the hardest crystal and talc is the softest.

Sometimes two crystals of the same size have very different weights. We say they have different **density**. For example, 1 cubic centimeter (3⁄5 cubic inch) of galena crystal is three times heavier than a talc crystal of the same size, so the galena is three times as dense.

The table below shows how the density and hardness of a range of crystals are clearly different.

Crystal	Color	Hardness (Mohs)	Density (g per cubic cm/ oz per cubic in.)
zirconia	varied	7.5	4.70 / 2.18
ruby	red	9.0	4.00 / 2.31
diamond	colorless	10.0	3.50 / 2.02
olivine	olive green	7.0	3.30 / 1.91
emerald	green	8.0	2.75 / 1.59
feldspar	varied	6.0	2.50 / 1.45
quartz	varied	7.0	2.50 / 1.45
opal	varied	7.0	2.00 / 1.16

HOW DO WE USE CRYSTALS?

We use different crystals for different things. Mixing them up could be dangerous, so we need to have ways to clearly identify them.

PASS THE SALT!

People use salt to flavor food, and a little salt also keeps us healthy. We get salt from seawater (see page 8) and also from hard **rock salt** in underground mines. Miners pump hot water through rock salt to **dissolve** the **minerals**. The salty **solution** is then **crystallized**. Rock salt is not just for food. People use salt on roads to melt ice during cold weather and to make chlorine to clean water, so that it is safe to drink.

A backhoe removes pieces of rock salt cut from salt mines in Germany. Pillars of rock salt remain on either side to hold the roof up!

WATCHES AND LASERS

Most crystals vibrate (shake) an exact number of times each second when electricity passes through them. **Quartz** watches convert the vibrations of quartz into movement of watch hands, or they use these vibrations to change the numbers on a watch display panel.

Crystals can also vibrate in strong light. For example, chromium **atoms** in ruby crystals produce red light when they vibrate. This can be turned into a thin beam of red light in a **laser**. Lasers using various crystals have many uses, from reading DVDs to cutting flesh in surgery!

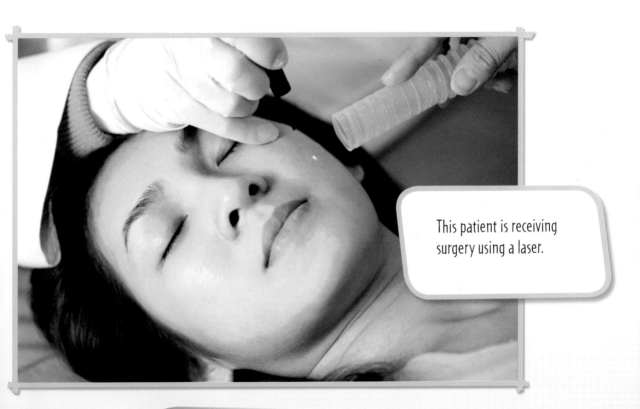

This patient is receiving surgery using a laser.

Biography
Theodore Maiman lived from 1927 to 2007. When he was young, he enjoyed taking radios apart and putting them back together. Later, in 1960, he invented the ruby laser. He intended for it to be used by doctors, but it was first used to measure the distance from Earth to the Moon!

PRECIOUS CRYSTALS

Some crystals are so beautiful and rare that people buy them as **gemstones** to make into jewelry and other decorative objects. Many, such as diamonds, rubies, and sapphires, are clear, but not all. For example, opal is a cloudy gemstone that contains lots of tiny crystals that produce different, shimmering colors.

The best-quality gemstones are usually big and intensely colored, and they reflect light very well. Most of these crystals look uninteresting when people find them in the ground. Jewelers use special saws to cut a pattern of flat faces called **facets** over the surface of gemstones. These facets can reflect light like mirrors in all directions.

A jeweler uses a magnifying glass to examine the **symmetry** of facets on a diamond gemstone.

CRYSTAL POWERS

People have long believed in the healing powers of crystals. Ancient Egyptians thought that red crystals could cure blood problems. Today, some people still think crystals have powers. For example, they put rose quartz crystals on their heads to soothe headaches and to calm down.

Science tip

Jewelers may polish crystals to make them smooth and shiny. Put a few rough crystals with half a cup each of sand and water into a plastic jar with a screw-on lid. Tape the lid on to stop water from spilling and shake the jar for as long as you can every day for two weeks. The crystals will be smoother because the sand has worn away the rough edges. This is why stones on a beach are smooth!

Artist Damien Hirst designed this metal skull covered in over 8,000 diamonds in 2007. The large gemstone on the forehead is worth $7 million by itself.

ARE CRYSTALS RUNNING OUT?

Many crystals we use today were formed millions of years ago. There are still huge quantities of crystals such as **gypsum** and **quartz**, but others are running out. For example, tanzanite may run out within 15 years. New crystals are gradually forming inside Earth, but it could take thousands of years for them to be revealed at the surface by **weathering** and **erosion**.

MINING PROBLEMS

When mines start to run out of crystals, mining companies dig in new places. Sometimes they cut down rain forests, build roads across deserts, and spoil other **ecosystems** to make new mines. They may make miners work in unsafe conditions and for low pay so that they can make more money from the crystals they sell.

Rock roles

Some **geologists** work for **fair-trade gemstone** groups. They make sure that crystal miners are paid fairly, work in safety, and do not damage the land they mine. Some of these geologists work in Africa to stop the mining of blood diamonds. These are diamonds sold by people who mistreat the miners and use the diamonds to pay for wars.

MINING WASTE

Mining for crystals leaves piles of waste rock on Earth's surface. Rainwater can react with the **minerals** in this rock to create **acid**. Acids can harm animals and plants that live in rivers and lakes. When gravel is sucked up from the seabed to find crystals, the fish and their eggs among the rocks are destroyed.

Another problem is that large holes form underground when crystals are removed. In some places the land surface, along with buildings and roads, collapses. This creates **sinkholes**. In 1994 in New York state, the biggest salt mine in the United States filled with water from underground. This **dissolved** enough **rock salt** for many sinkholes to form, some the length of a soccer field!

Acids from mining can end up in rivers and damage wildlife.

GROW YOUR OWN CRYSTALS!

Grow crystal **stalactites** on a piece of yarn! Choose a dry, warm room to speed up **crystallization**.

YOU WILL NEED:

- two glass jars
- a saucer
- a jug containing half a liter (1 pint) of hot tap water
- a teaspoon
- two paper clips
- 1-meter (3-foot) piece of white yarn
- baking soda
- food coloring.

WHAT TO DO:

1. Fold the yarn in half and in half again. Twist the yarn tightly.

2. Dangle one end of the yarn into each glass jar and weigh down the ends with paper clips so that the yarn forms a shallow curve between the jars. Place the saucer between the jars.

3. Keep stirring teaspoons of the baking soda into the jug of water until no more **dissolves**. Add 10–20 drops of food coloring. Pour enough of this **solution** into each jar to reach the yarn.

4. Wet the yarn with water and watch the solution gradually soak through the yarn. If a pool of solution forms on the saucer, tip it back in the jars. Do not touch the yarn for several days.

5. Crystals should start to form on the yarn in about two days. Fill up the jars with any extra solution as it becomes used up for crystallization. Stalactites should start to grow down from the bottom of the yarn curve in about a week.

Science tips

Crystals of baking soda grow slowly when there is a constant supply of strong **mineral** solution. Spaces between the fibers of wool in the yarn are good, damp places for **seed crystals** to form.

GLOSSARY

acid substance, usually liquid, that can damage things it touches if very strong

acidic when a substance contains a lot of acid

atom smallest particle of chemical matter that can exist

calcite type of mineral found in limestone rock

core central part of Earth

crust rocky surface layer of Earth

crystallization process during which crystals are formed from minerals or other substances

crystallize form crystals from minerals or other substances

crystallographer scientist who studies crystal structure and properties

density measure of mass in a given volume of a substance. For example, rock is denser than air.

dissolve completely mix with a liquid

ecosystem living things and the environment they live in

erosion wearing away of rocks by flowing water, wind, and glaciers

evaporation process of changing from a liquid into a gas

facet flat side of a gemstone

fair trade trade that makes sure workers have fair pay and working conditions

feldspar type of white or red mineral commonly found in rocks

gemstone precious stone that has been cut and polished and used to make jewelry

geologist scientist who studies the rocks and soil from which Earth is made

graphite soft, black mineral that is used to make pencils and other items

gypsum soft, white mineral like chalk. Gypsum is used to make plaster.

laser device that concentrates light into an intense, narrow beam

magma hot liquid rock below Earth's crust

mantle very deep layer of hot rock below Earth's crust

mineral substance that is naturally present in Earth, such as gold and salt

molecule group of atoms

particle tiny piece

pressure force or weight pushing against something

quartz hard mineral, often found in crystal form

rock cycle constant formation, destruction, and recycling of rocks through Earth's crust

rock salt hard natural rock made of salt crystals

sedimentary rock type of rock formed from tiny pieces of rock or shells of sea animals

seed crystal tiny single crystal from which a larger crystal grows

silicon one of the most common elements in Earth's crust, found in rocks and sand

sinkhole crater in the land caused by the collapse of the roof of a cave (or when the limestone holding it up dissolves)

solution liquid in which a substance is dissolved

stalactite long, pointed rock hanging down from the roof of a cave

stalagmite long, pointed rock growing up from the floor of a cave

sulfur pale yellow element

symmetrical when both sides of a thing are exactly the same size and shape

symmetry having two sides exactly the same size and shape but the opposite way around, as if one were a mirror image of the other

vein thin layer of minerals or metal found within rock

volcano opening in Earth's surface where magma escapes from underground

weathering breaking up of rock by weather conditions such as extremes of temperature

X-ray type of light that can pass

FIND OUT MORE

BOOKS

Faulkner, Rebecca. *Crystals* (Geology Rocks!). Chicago: Raintree, 2008.

Pellant, Chris, and Helen Pellant. *Crystals and Gemstones* (Gareth Stevens Learning Library). Pleasantville, N.Y.: Gareth Stevens, 2009.

Symes, R. F., and R. R. Harding. *Crystal and Gem* (Eyewitness). New York: Dorling Kindersley, 2007.

WEBSITES

Try another crystal-growing experiment at:
www.exploratorium.edu/science_explorer/crystal.html

Find out more about the giant crystal caves in Mexico at:
http://channel.nationalgeographic.com/series/naked-science /3569/Overview

PLACES TO VISIT

American Museum of Natural History
Central Park West at 79th Street
New York, New York, 10024-5192
Tel: (212) 769-5100
www.amnh.org
Visit the museum's Hall of Minerals and Gems.

The Field Museum
1400 S. Lake Shore Drive
Chicago, Illinois 60605-2496
Tel: (312) 922-9410
www.fieldmuseum.org
Check out exhibits of rocks, minerals, and fossils from around the world.

INDEX